This Guest Book Celebrates

RETIREMENT!

D1736658

Retirement Guest Book

Name	Message

Retirement Guest Book

Name

Message

Retirement Guest Book

Name

Message

Retirement Guest Book

Name   Message

Retirement Guest Book

Name

Message

Retirement Guest Book

Name

Message

Retirement Guest Book

Name

Message

Retirement Guest Book

Name   Message

Retirement Guest Book

Name

Message

Retirement Guest Book

Name　　　　　　　　　　　　　　　Message

Retirement Guest Book

Name

Message

Retirement Guest Book

Name   Message

Retirement Guest Book

Name

Message

Retirement Guest Book

Name

Message

Retirement Guest Book

Name

Message

Retirement Guest Book

Name

Message

Retirement Guest Book

Name

Message

Retirement Guest Book

Name

Message

Retirement Guest Book

Name

Message

Retirement Guest Book

Name   Message

Retirement Guest Book

Name

Message

Retirement Guest Book

Name   Message

Retirement Guest Book

Name   Message

Retirement Guest Book

Name   Message

Retirement Guest Book

Name

Message

Retirement Guest Book

Name   Message

Retirement Guest Book

Name

Message

Retirement Guest Book

Name

Message

Retirement Guest Book

Name

Message

Retirement Guest Book

Name

Message

Retirement Guest Book

Name

Message

Retirement Guest Book

Name   Message

Retirement Guest Book

Name	Message

Retirement Guest Book

Name   Message

Retirement Guest Book

Name   Message

Retirement Guest Book

Name

Message

Retirement Guest Book

Name

Message

Retirement Guest Book

Name

Message

Retirement Guest Book

Name

Message

Retirement Guest Book

Name   Message

Retirement Guest Book

Name

Message

Retirement Guest Book

Name

Message

Retirement Guest Book

Name   Message

Retirement Guest Book

Name   Message

Retirement Guest Book

Name

Message

Retirement Guest Book

Name

Message

Retirement Guest Book

Name   Message

Retirement Guest Book

Name

Message

Retirement Guest Book

Name

Message

Retirement Guest Book

Name

Message

Retirement Guest Book

Name	Message

Retirement Guest Book

Name

Message

Retirement Guest Book

Name

Message

Retirement Guest Book

Name

Message

Retirement Guest Book

Name

Message

Retirement Guest Book

Name   Message

Retirement Guest Book

Name

Message

Retirement Guest Book

Name   **Message**

Retirement Guest Book

Name

Message

Retirement Guest Book

Name

Message

Retirement Guest Book

Name   Message

Retirement Guest Book

Name   Message

Retirement Guest Book

Name   Message

Retirement Guest Book

Name   Message

Retirement Guest Book

Name

Message

Retirement Guest Book

Name

Message

Retirement Guest Book

Name   Message

Retirement Guest Book

Name

Message

Retirement Guest Book

Name

Message

Retirement Guest Book

Name

Message

Retirement Guest Book

Name   Message

Retirement Guest Book

Name

Message

Retirement Guest Book

Name	Message

Retirement Guest Book

Name

Message

Retirement Guest Book

Name

Message

Retirement Guest Book

Name

Message

Retirement Guest Book

Name

Message

Retirement Guest Book

Name	Message

Retirement Guest Book

Name

Message

Retirement Guest Book

Name

Message

Retirement Guest Book

Name   Message

Retirement Guest Book

Name	Message

Retirement Guest Book

Name

Message

Retirement Guest Book

Name   Message

Retirement Guest Book

Name   Message

Retirement Guest Book

Name

Message

Retirement Guest Book

Name

Message

Retirement Guest Book

Name   Message

Retirement Guest Book

Name

Message

Retirement Guest Book

Name

Message

Retirement Guest Book

Name

Message

Retirement Guest Book

Name

Message

Retirement Guest Book

Name

Message

Retirement Guest Book

Name

Message

Retirement Guest Book

Name

Message

Retirement Guest Book

Name

Message

Retirement Guest Book

Name

Message

Retirement Guest Book

Name

Message

Retirement Guest Book

Name

Message

Retirement Guest Book

Name

Message

Retirement Guest Book

Name

Message

Retirement Guest Book

Name   Message

Retirement Guest Book

Name

Message

Retirement Guest Book

Name

Message

Retirement Guest Book

Name

Message

Retirement Guest Book

Name

Message

Retirement Guest Book

Name

Message

Retirement Guest Book

Name

Message

Retirement Guest Book

Name | Message

Retirement Guest Book

Name

Message

Retirement Guest Book

Name

Message

Retirement Guest Book

Name	Message

Retirement Guest Book

Name

Message

Retirement Guest Book

Name

Message

Retirement Guest Book

Name

Message

Retirement Guest Book

Name   Message

Retirement Guest Book

Name   Message

Retirement Guest Book

Name

Message

Retirement Guest Book

Name

Message

Retirement Guest Book

Name

Message

Made in the USA
Las Vegas, NV
23 August 2023

76510722R00070